Great Group Games

FOR YOUTH MINISTRY

Group®

Loveland, Colorado

Contributors
Michael Warden, Stephen Parolini, Rick Lawrence, and Michael Capps

Credits
Edited by Michael Warden
Cover designed by Liz Howe and Diana Walters
Interior designed by Lisa Smith
Illustrations contributed by Elizabeth Woodworth

Library of Congress Cataloging-in-Publication Data
Great group games for youth ministry / [contributors, Michael Warden ... et al.].
   p.   cm.
   ISBN 1-55945-186-6 :
   1. Church group work with teenagers. 2. Games in Christian education.   I. Warden, Michael D.
BV4447.G66   1994
259' .23--dc20   93-35768
                                  CIP

11 10 9 8 7 6   03 02 01 00 99 98

Printed in the United States of America

⬛ Contents

INTRODUCTION

GAMES FOR SMALL PLACES

Games to play in your meeting room or any small indoor location.

GAMES FOR GREAT HALLS

Games to play in any large indoor space, such as a gymnasium, auditorium, or fellowship hall.

GAMES ON THE GO

Games to play in various locations or in a vehicle en route to those locations.

GAMES FOR THE GREAT OUTDOORS

Games to play in various outdoor locations such as parks, sport fields, wooded areas, or swimming pools.

GAMES FOR ALL KINDS OF WEATHER

Games to play when it's raining, snowing, or blowing outside.

Introduction

If you're like most youth workers, you're always looking for fun, new, and innovative games to play with your kids. You've probably grown tired of the old standby games, such as Killer (wink, wink) or the ever-so-ancient Charades. You (not to mention your youth group!) are probably ready for a change.

Well, we've got good news! *Great Group Games for Youth Ministry* is packed with over 90 new and innovative games you and your kids will love. Fresh ideas. New twists. Really *fun* games!

Whether your group has two young people or 202, *Great Group Games for Youth Ministry* is packed with easy-to-use games for all sorts of occasions. Take a look at the variety of games we've included:

- **Games for Small Places—**These games can be played in your meeting room or in another small, indoor location.
- **Games for Great Halls—**These games work well in gymnasiums, auditoriums, fellowship halls, or any other vast indoor space.
- **Games on the Go—**These are games you can play at various locations around town or in a vehicle en route to those locations.
- **Games for the Great Outdoors—**Play these games in various outdoor locations, such as parks, sports fields, swimming pools, lakes, or local neighborhoods.
- **Games for All Kinds of Weather—**This special section includes games that take advantage of weather conditions. Whether it's raining, snowing, or blowing outside, there are still games to be played. And we've got them.

In addition, the games are outlined so you know at a glance how many people are required to play each game—and what supplies are needed. Just about all the games can be easily adjusted to fit any size group. They're not only fun; they're convenient!

So, enjoy *Great Group Games for Youth Ministry*. Try a few of the games on your kids this week. You'll be glad you did.

And so will they.

Games for Small Places

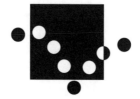

Balloon Blowout

Give each person seven balloons and a supply of string cut in 24-inch lengths. Have kids each blow up their balloons, tie each balloon to a length of string, and then tie the strings to their bodies or clothes. For example, they could tie a balloon on their waist, neck, backside, each ankle, and each wrist. Tell kids the object of the game is to pop all the balloons you can without letting any of your own balloons be popped. The only rule is that kids may not use their hands, feet, or teeth.

Clear an open space in the center of the room, then start the game. The last person with one or more balloons left unpopped wins.

● **PLAYERS:**

4 OR MORE

● **SUPPLIES:**

STRING, SCISSORS, AND SEVEN BAL-LOONS FOR EACH PERSON.

GAMES FOR SMALL PLACES

Belly-Flop and Pop

● PLAYERS:

10 OR MORE

● SUPPLIES:

ONE BAG OF RED BALLOONS AND ONE BAG OF BLUE BALLOONS.

Form two teams and assign each team a color—red or blue. Have kids blow up and tie off all the balloons, then spread them out on the floor. Tell kids the object of the game is to pop all the other team's balloons before they pop all of yours. The only rule is that balloons can be popped only by belly-flopping on them—no hands or feet allowed.

Start the game. The first team to belly-flop and pop all the other team's balloons wins.

■ Leader Tip:

In case some of your members don't feel comfortable belly-flopping on balloons, adjust the game to allow people to pop balloons by sitting on them.

·Bouncers

Get either a muffin tin or an empty egg carton. On the inside of each cup, write a point score ranging from 10 to 50. Place the muffin tin or the egg carton on the floor in an uncarpeted room.

Form two teams (a team can be one person). Give each team four or five Ping-Pong balls, then establish a throw line roughly five feet away from the carton or tin. Play the game as you would darts, except tell kids their Ping-Pong balls must each bounce once on the floor before landing in the tin or carton. After the first player has bounced his or her Ping-Pong balls, tally the score and attribute it to his or her team.

The team with the highest score after three rounds wins.

● **PLAYERS:**

2 OR MORE

● **SUPPLIES:**

A MUFFIN TIN OR EGG CARTON, A MARKER, AND 10 PING-PONG BALLS.

GAMES FOR SMALL PLACES

Copycat

● PLAYERS:

2 OR MORE

● SUPPLIES:

NONE NEEDED.

Form a circle. One at a time, have kids each perform an action for the rest of the group to copy. Anyone who can't or won't copy the action must leave the circle. The object of the game is to be the last person left in the circle—so encourage kids to choose actions that not everyone can do (such as touching your tongue to your nose). Offer a prize to the winner to motivate people to keep trying to "copycat."

■ Leader Tip:

This game works as a great discussion starter on what kids are willing to do to be accepted—and what happens to those who can't "perform" as well as others.

⬛·Don't Say It!

Form teams of four. Assign each group a different topic, such as school, sports, television, movies, food, or church; then have them each come up with a list of 10 words relating to their topic. Tell kids they can't include simple words such as "the" or "it" and that the words must be common in conversations about the topic. For example, a list for sports might include "game," "winner," "play," "ball," "out," "athlete," "field," and "inning."

Have each team give its list to you. Then, one at a time, have teams each talk for two minutes about a topic (not their own) that was used for creating one of the lists. Have each team member talk for 30 seconds about his or her experience with that particular topic. Each time someone says one of the key words, discretely make a mark on the list. A point is scored for the list-making team each time a word on its list is used. Use your judgment on variations of specific words.

Play this game until each team has talked about a particular topic. The team with the most points in the end wins.

● **PLAYERS:**

8 OR MORE

● **SUPPLIES:**

PAPER AND PEN-CILS.

GAMES FOR SMALL PLACES

⬛·Fake Forms

● PLAYERS:

4 OR MORE

● SUPPLIES:

BLANK EMPLOY-
MENT APPLICA-
TIONS AND PEN-
CILS.

Get photocopies of employment application forms from a local business and
use correction fluid to delete any reference
to the actual business. Form pairs or trios
and give each group one or two of the
forms. Have kids work together to create
fake applications based on popular fictional
or historical characters. Encourage kids to
have fun with the "previous work experience" section as well as the "history of
education" section.

For example, a form for Albert Einstein
might list "the speed of light" as an area of
expertise and "thinking up theories" as a
hobby. Have group members also put their
names on their forms.

When the forms are complete, collect
them and give each team a blank form to
look at during the game. Pull out a fake
application, then have one of the teams
pick any portion of the form for you to
read aloud (except the name, of course).
See if team members can guess the character based only on the information in that
portion. Continue until one of the teams
guesses the character. Repeat this until
teams have guessed the identities of all the
characters listed on the forms (except their
own, of course). The team that guesses the
most characters wins.

■ Leader Tip:

To help kids learn more about Bible
characters, limit the choices to biblical per-
sonalities.

● GREAT GROUP GAMES

Flame Blower

Tell kids the goal of this game is simple—to be the first person to drink your glass of water. The only rule is that you can drink from your glass only while your candle is lit. Tell kids they must try to blow out their opponents' candles while keeping their own lit so they can drink their water.

Have kids light their candles, then begin the game. The first person to finish his or her glass of water wins.

■ Leader Tip:

Remind kids to use their candles and matches safely. Tell them to be careful not to jostle the table, or they might knock a flame onto the floor.

Also, you can include more people in this game by creating a tournament setup, in which kids move from table to table according to whether they win or lose.

● PLAYERS:

4 OR FEWER

● SUPPLIES:

FOR EACH PERSON, YOU'LL NEED A FREE-STANDING CANDLE, A BOX OF MATCHES, AND A GLASS OF WATER. YOU'LL ALSO NEED A SQUARE CARD TABLE.

GAMES FOR SMALL PLACES

Hat Hoops

● **PLAYERS:**

10 OR MORE

● **SUPPLIES:**

TWO BASEBALL CAPS AND A LARGE WAD OF PAPER OR ALUMINUM FOIL.

Form two teams and have kids from different teams spread themselves evenly among chairs lined up like a van or bus. Give one person on each team a baseball cap. These people will start out as the "baskets." A crumpled sheet of paper or a wad of aluminum foil will be the ball in this game.

Say: **The object of this game is to get the ball into your opponent's hat. The hat holders—or baskets— must hold the hats in the air and not move them at all. All team members may use only the hand they don't write with during this game—put the other hand behind your back.**

While sitting in your seats, you may pass the ball to a teammate or attempt a shot at the basket. You may not grab the ball from another person or touch others in any way. If your pass or shot hits the floor, the other team gets the ball. Any violation of the rules will result in a free throw for the opposing team.

Rotate who plays the part of the baskets after each score. Play to a predetermined point goal or time limit.

Instant Replays

Form teams of four. Place four chairs in a line at one end of the room. Choose a team to create the first "people sculpture." Then have everyone else look away from the team or close their eyes.

Allow one minute for the people-sculpture team to arrange themselves any way they choose on the chairs (including where each person sits or stands, where they place their arms and legs, and what expressions they wear).

Once they're arranged, have everyone else turn and look at the sculpture for exactly 15 seconds. During this time, take an instant-print photograph of the people sculpture. At the end of 15 seconds, call time and have everyone turn back around so they can't see the sculpture.

Allow the people-sculpture team to rearrange themselves in any way they choose (changing seats, position of legs and arms, expressions, and so on). After one minute, have everyone else turn around and work together to arrange the sculpture back into its original form. Encourage each person to add suggestions so they'll get as close to the original as possible.

When they think they have it (or after about three minutes), call time and compare the current sculpture with the photograph. Give teams each a chance to be the people sculpture.

● **PLAYERS:**

8 OR MORE

● **SUPPLIES:**

AN INSTANT-PRINT CAMERA.

GAMES FOR SMALL PLACES

Lights On– Lights Off

● **PLAYERS:**

2 OR MORE

● **SUPPLIES:**

NONE NEEDED.

The object of the game is to follow the instructions of the leader and not get caught making a mistake.

To begin the game, choose a leader and have him or her stand by the light switch. The leader then decides on two actions—one for the command "lights on" and the other for the command "lights off." For example, a leader might choose jumping jacks for "lights on" and flapping your arms like a chicken for "lights off."

Whenever the leader says, "Lights on," kids must do the appropriate action. Likewise, when the leader says, "Lights off," the kids must switch to the other action. The catch is that during this time, the leader also turns the lights on and off at random. Anyone caught doing the wrong action at any time is out. The last person in wins the game.

■ **Leader Tip:**

To add to the confusion, have the leader call out bogus commands such as "switch actions" or "change now" to trick kids into doing the wrong action. Remind kids that only the commands "lights on" and "lights off" are valid.

Overhead Relays

Form two teams and arrange each team in a line, with kids all facing toward one end of the line. Give the last person in each line an assortment of items from the supply list. The items don't have to be identical for each team, but teams each must have the same number of items.

Say: **In this relay race, the goal is to pass all the objects from the back of the line to the front by tossing them one at a time over the head of the person in front of you. No one may turn around or speak at any time, and any dropped item must be returned to the end of the line and restarted. The first team to successfully pass all its items to the front of the line wins.**

Start the game. Monitor kids to make sure no one turns around or talks during the game (all other sounds are OK). When the first round is over, mix up the teams and play again—or keep the same teams and play two out of three.

● **PLAYERS:**

8 OR MORE

● **SUPPLIES:**

AN ASSORTMENT OF SMALL ITEMS— SUCH AS A PING- PONG BALL, A SET OF KEYS, A PENCIL, AND A SOCK.

used 9-99

GAMES FOR SMALL PLACES

Pavlovian Charades

• PLAYERS:

4 OR MORE

• SUPPLIES:

THREE BAGS OF M&M'S, PAPER, AND PENCILS.

Form two teams (a team can be as few as two people). Give each team a bag of M&M's, paper, and pencils. On their paper, have teams each come up with a list of four or five actions for the opposing team to perform. The actions need to be simple, but they can be unusual; for example, "sit cross-legged on the floor and stick both thumbs in your mouth" or "stand on one leg and flap your arms like a chicken."

Once teams have finished their lists, explain how Pavlovian Charades works. Each member of the opposing team will be given one or more of the actions your team created. That person's job is to get his or her teammates to perform the action without speaking or gesturing in any way. All he or she can do is place an M&M's piece in the mouth of any team member who makes a move toward performing the action.

For example, if the action calls for team members to stick their thumbs in their mouths, then the person with the M&M's can award one to any person who lifts a hand to his or her face. It's up to team members to decide what behavior is being rewarded and to act accordingly. The charade is over only when all the team members have performed the action.

Give 1 point to each team that completes the action within five minutes. At the end, award the winning team with a bag of M&M's.

• **GREAT GROUP GAMES**

Puzzle Twister

Before this game, create a huge puzzle out of cardboard with four times as many pieces as there are kids in your group. The puzzle pieces should each be 1- to 3-feet square, and they should have no markings on them. Create string straps for each piece so the pieces can be slipped onto kids' feet and hands.

Mix up the pieces and give four to each group member. Have kids mill around and swap pieces until they believe they can all position their bodies to complete the puzzle when they slip their puzzle pieces on their feet and hands. Give kids only a couple of minutes to swap pieces and choose which foot and hand each piece will be placed on. Then have kids attempt to complete the puzzle by positioning themselves so puzzle pieces connect.

If kids can't finish the puzzle on the first try, give them another two minutes to swap pieces or move them from hand to foot or foot to hand.

■ Leader Tip:

For a more competitive version of this game, create two identical puzzles, then form two teams and have them race to see which one can complete the puzzle first.

GAMES FOR SMALL PLACES

Racing Eights

• PLAYERS:

8 OR MORE

• SUPPLIES:

CONFETTI, WATER, AND A CUP FOR EACH PERSON.

Choose a room where it's OK if water spills on the floor. Form a figure eight with the chairs in that room and have kids sit on them. Give one person a cup filled with confetti and each of the rest of the people an empty cup. On "go," have kids (except for the person holding the cup of confetti) hold their cups behind their heads. Have the person with the confetti-filled cup pour the confetti into the cup in front of him or her. Continue this process until the confetti is returned to the original holder's cup.

Then, pour water into the cup of the person who's farthest away from the confetti-cup holder. On "go," have kids cause the water to "chase" the confetti around the circle. The game is over when:

- the water catches the confetti (which, by the way, is theoretically impossible),
- the water is all spilled, or
- the confetti is all spilled.

■ Leader Tip:

This activity gets messy, so you'll need a vacuum cleaner and towels handy for cleaning up.

Shoe Quest

Before kids enter the meeting room, have them remove their shoes and place them in a large can or plastic trash bag. Place the shoes in a separate room adjacent to the meeting room. Once everyone has arrived, form pairs and have one person in each pair become the "runner." Tell kids that the object of the game is for the runner to get a description of his or her partner's shoes, run to the "shoe room," retrieve the shoes, and then put them on his or her partner's feet.

On "go," runners each get the description of the shoes and run to retrieve them. Of course, if they get the wrong pair, they must return the shoes and try again. The first pair to complete the task wins. After the first round, return all the shoes to the shoe room and have partners switch roles. Then play the game again.

● PLAYERS:

10 OR MORE

● SUPPLIES:

EVERYONE'S SHOES AND A TRASH BAG OR LARGE CAN.

GAMES FOR SMALL PLACES

Silent-Message Relay Race

● **PLAYERS:**

8 OR MORE

● **SUPPLIES:**

NONE NEEDED.

Form two teams and have them each form a line, with kids facing the front of the line. Choose a simple message to give to the last person in the line; for example, "I am sleepy" or "He is tall." Tell kids the object of the game is to get your message to the front of the line by conveying it nonverbally to the person in front of you.

Tell kids they can turn around only when they're receiving the message from the person behind them. At all other times, they must face the front of the line. Kids can use any means they want to convey the message. The only rules are that they may not speak and that they may not leave the line.

Whisper the message to the last person on each team, then start the race. The first team to transfer the correct message to the first person in line wins.

Surprises in Disguises

orm two teams. Give teams each a set of disguise items, then send them into separate rooms. Tell kids the goal of the game is to disguise one of their members so that the other team can't tell who it is. Have teams each choose a person to disguise, then use the supplies to mask his or her true identity.

When teams are ready, have them each send their disguised person into the other team's room. That team may look closely at the disguised person, but no touching is allowed. If the team guesses the person's identity, that teams get a point. If they guess incorrectly, the other team gets a point. Continue the game until each person has had a chance to be disguised. The team with the most points at the end of the game wins.

● **PLAYERS:**

6 OR MORE

● **SUPPLIES:**

TWO SETS OF ITEMS THAT CAN BE USED TO CREATE A DISGUISE—SUCH AS WIGS, SUNGLASSES, FAKE BEARDS, HATS, TRENCH COATS, SHEETS, AND SO ON.

GAMES FOR SMALL PLACES

Time to Win

● PLAYERS:

4 OR MORE

● SUPPLIES:

PAPER, PENCILS, AND A STOP-WATCH.

Form teams of two to four. Create a list of activities for groups to do; for example, stack 20 items in a tower, wash the windows of three cars in the parking lot, tap dance the theme to a popular movie, scratch each person's back, and so on.

Assign an activity to each group, then have groups decide how long they think it will take to complete the activity (in minutes and seconds). Using a stopwatch to time the groups, have them each perform their activity and return to a predetermined "base" when they're finished.

Play loud music while kids perform the activities and don't let them wear watches or look at clocks to time themselves. Give teams each 1 point for every second they either overshot or undershot their predicted time. The team with the lowest score at the end of three rounds wins.

Toilet Paper Pieces Race

Form teams of four and give each team one square of toilet paper. Set up a short racecourse through the meeting room by arranging chairs to form the boundaries of a curving track. Explain that the goal of the race is to move your square of toilet paper from the start to the finish line *without touching it*. Team members must use their breath to keep the toilet paper airborne through the entire course. Tell kids they may also sabotage other teams' efforts by blowing their toilet paper squares off course, but their first priority is to keep their own toilet paper square afloat.

Line up teams at the starting line, then begin the race. The first team to successfully blow its piece across the finish line wins.

● **PLAYERS:**

8 OR MORE

● **SUPPLIES:**

TOILET PAPER.

GAMES FOR SMALL PLACES

⬛ Toilet Paper Relay Run

● PLAYERS:

6 OR MORE

● SUPPLIES:

TWO ROLLS OF TOILET PAPER.

Form two teams and have teams form two lines, side by side, at one end of the room. Designate a line at the other end of the room as the finish line. Direct team members to stand with their legs apart, facing the finish line. Give the first person in each line a roll of toilet paper.

Say: **The goal of the game is to wrap the toilet paper around your teammates' ankles, then race to the finish line without breaking the strand. You can wrap the toilet paper however you wish, as long as each of your ankles has been wrapped with toilet paper at least once. Also, at all times during the race, you must remain at least an arm's length away from the person in front of you and behind you. If at any time during the race your strand breaks, your team must return to the beginning, rewrap the toilet paper, and start again.**

Start the race. The first team to successfully cross the finish line wins.

Watch My Back

Form pairs. Give kids each a handkerchief and have them tuck the handkerchiefs under their collars behind their necks. Then have pairs lock arms, back to back.

Tell kids the object of the game is to steal as many handkerchiefs as they can while keeping their own handkerchiefs from being stolen. Pairs must keep one set of arms locked at all times. As handkerchiefs are stolen, they must be placed in the collar of the person who stole them. Pairs are "out" when both of their handkerchiefs have been stolen. The pair with the most handkerchiefs in the end wins.

● **PLAYERS:**

4 OR MORE

● **SUPPLIES:**

A HANDKERCHIEF FOR EACH PERSON.

GAMES FOR SMALL PLACES

⬛·Whose Izzit?

Have kids each bring from home one personal item that represents a hobby or interest they have. For example, a tennis racquet or a baseball glove might show a group member's interest in sports. Tell kids to hide their items in paper bags.

In the meeting room, mix up the bags and set them on the floor in a circle. Have kids form a circle around the bags, each facing a bag (not their own). Choose someone to go first and have that person peek in the bag next to him or her, then silently guess who the item belongs to. Then have that person direct the group to rotate clockwise until the person he or she has chosen is positioned in front of the first bag.

Then have the person to the right of the first person peek inside the bag next to him or her and locate the person he or she thinks the item in the bag belongs to. Have the group rotate again, excluding the person positioned in front of the first bag.

Continue until the last person in the line is facing the last bag (whether or not it's that person's bag). Then have kids each pull out their items and say whether or not it's theirs. If it is theirs, have them tell what it represents. If the item isn't theirs, have the group vote on who the item might belong to, then have the real owner claim the item and explain what it represents.

● GREAT GROUP GAMES

ᐧᐧᐧᐧContagion

Form a circle and have one volunteer leave the room. Assign one person in the circle to be the leader. Tell the group to mimic whatever the leader does but, at the same time, to keep the leader's identity a secret. Tell the leader to quietly lead the group to do simple actions, such as placing their hands on their hips, scratching their necks, or snapping their fingers to a beat.

Bring the volunteer back into the room and have him or her stand in the center of the circle. Tell the volunteer that the goal is to identify the leader within two minutes.

Start the game. As soon as the volunteer has identified the leader, have him or her pick a new volunteer to leave the room. Then pick a new leader and start the game again.

● **PLAYERS:**

10 OR MORE

● **SUPPLIES:**

NONE NEEDED.

GAMES FOR SMALL PLACES

Blind Leading the Blind

● PLAYERS:

10 OR MORE

● SUPPLIES:

A BLINDFOLD FOR EACH PERSON.

Form two teams, then blindfold each person. On "go," have teams race to line up alphabetically according to first name. The first team to form the line correctly wins the round. Hold two more rounds, using these parameters:

● Have teams line up by birthdays.

● Have teams line up by the color of their outfits (brightest to darkest).

The team that wins the most rounds wins the game.

Games for Great Halls

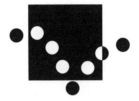

Blind Chalice Quest

● PLAYERS:

8 OR MORE

● SUPPLIES:

A CUP OR GLASS AND ONE BLIND-FOLD FOR EVERY FOUR PEOPLE.

Form teams of four and choose one person from each team to blindfold. Show kids your "chalice"—a cup or a glass—and place it in an obscure but reachable part of the room. Line up all the teams behind a line at the opposite end of the room. On "go," have teams each race to get the chalice by directing their blindfolded teammate to the object. Tell kids they may give verbal directions only—no touching allowed. Allow kids the option of assigning one or more of their team members to run "interference" on the other teams by giving bogus commands to blindfolded racers.

The first team to retrieve the chalice wins. Play several rounds, allowing different people to be blindfolded each time.

Broom-Hockey Face Off

Form two teams and have them line up on opposite sides of the gym. Establish two goals—one on each end of the room—and assign one to each team. Set out the two brooms and the eraser in the center of the room. Have team members number off.

Explain that Broom-Hockey Face Off works like regular broom hockey, except that only two players play at a time. Tell kids you'll call out two numbers at random—the first number corresponds to a player on the first team, while the second number corresponds to a player on the second team. Once you call out both numbers, those two players race to the brooms and begin playing, each trying to knock the eraser into his or her assigned goal. Every 15 to 30 seconds, call out another pair of numbers. Once the new numbers are called, the old players drop their brooms and make room for the new players, who're racing to pick up the brooms and continue the game. No broom "handoffs" are allowed.

Keep score and play until everyone has had at least two chances to play. The team with the most points at the end wins.

● PLAYERS:

10 OR MORE

● SUPPLIES:

TWO BROOMS AND A CHALKBOARD ERASER.

Fill-'Er-Up

● **PLAYERS:**

4 OR MORE

● **SUPPLIES:**

AN ASSORTMENT OF DIFFERENT-SIZED BALLS (SUCH AS BASKETBALLS, TENNIS BALLS, PLAYGROUND BALLS, FOOTBALLS, VOLLEYBALLS, AND SOFTBALLS). YOU'LL ALSO NEED A MESH-TYPE LAUNDRY BAG.

Use a gymnasium with a basketball hoop for this game. Before the game, have kids help you attach a mesh-type laundry bag to the basketball net or rim. It should be secure enough to withstand the pressure of a ball being thrown into it.

Form two teams. Designate four or five different shooting locations around the room and determine a point value for each one (the harder the shot, the more the points).

Tell teams the goal is to maximize their point earnings by using the most difficult shooting locations to get as many balls as possible into the bag before it fills up.

Once teams have each developed a game plan, have opposing team players take turns shooting the balls from the various shooting locations. Call time when the laundry bag is full. The team with the most points when you call time wins.

Fruit Roll-Up

Play this game in a large, carpeted room. Have kids each bring a large, plastic garbage bag from home. Lay the bags end to end and tape them together using duct tape on both sides. The end result should be a long line of bags that stretches across the room. Challenge your kids to see how many people they can roll up in the garbage-bag line.

Here's how it works: Have the first person lie down across one end of the line, grab the end of the plastic, and roll toward the other end. Make sure kids don't put the plastic over their faces. After one revolution, the first person should be wrapped in plastic. Then have the next person lie down on the plastic. Have the first person crawl over and lie down on the other side of the second person. At this point, both kids will be wrapped in plastic. Keep adding kids until you've run out of plastic, then have kids unroll as fast as they can.

■ Leader Tip:

For a competitive version of this game, form teams and have each team create the same size garbage-bag line. Then have teams compete to see which can roll all its members into the line first.

● **PLAYERS:**

10 OR MORE

● **SUPPLIES:**

DUCT TAPE AND A LARGE, PLASTIC GARBAGE BAG FOR EACH PERSON.

GAMES FOR GREAT HALLS

Giant Towers of Doom

● **PLAYERS:**

4 OR MORE

● **SUPPLIES:**

SEVERAL LARGE BOXES (LARGE APPLIANCE BOXES WORK BEST), A FEW SMALLER BOXES, MASKING TAPE, AND DUCT TAPE. YOU'LL ALSO NEED 20 TO 30 LIGHT, PLASTIC BASEBALLS.

Form two or three teams and give each team the same number of boxes. Have teams create towers at least 10 feet high using the big boxes and tape. Space the towers apart by designating a 10-foot diameter circle for each group to work in (you may use masking tape to mark off the circle). Encourage groups to make their towers secure.

Then, have groups each place a smaller box (same size for each group) on top of their towers. This box will be known as the "king." Give groups each a supply of 10 light, plastic baseballs.

Say: **The object of this game is to knock down the opposing teams' kings or towers, while protecting your own. You may not leave your own circle to throw the balls, and you may not touch your own tower to keep it standing. If your king is knocked off, the throwing team gets 1 point. You may then place the king on top of your tower again. If your tower is toppled, the throwing team gets 5 points. You may throw only 10 balls during each round.**

Play three rounds of three minutes each. Allow teams to "shore up" their towers between rounds. The team with the most points at the end of three rounds wins.

Hula Ball

Before the game, hang a Hula Hoop from the ceiling of a large hall so the bottom of the hoop is at least nine feet from the floor. Use a strong rope to attach the hoop to the ceiling so it can withstand lots of abuse. Then use masking tape to draw a 6-foot diameter circle on the floor below the hoop.

Form two teams. Give one person on each team a broom handle. These people will be the goalies. They must stand just outside the circle and defend the goal (the Hula Hoop) from their opponents—or attempt to tip a ball into the goal if shot by a teammate.

Then give each team a beach ball. On "go," teams must pass the balls around and attempt to throw them through the hoop. Goalies may block the shots with the broom handles, but they may not step more than one foot away from the circle. No one may enter the circle. Tell kids that they can move around but that no one may take more than two steps before either passing or shooting the ball.

Have a volunteer help you keep track of the score. The first team to score 15 goals wins.

■ Leader Tip:

Give kids each a chance to be goalie for their team.

● **PLAYERS:**

6 OR MORE

● **SUPPLIES:**

MASKING TAPE, A HULA HOOP, ROPE, A BEACH BALL, AND TWO BROOM HANDLES.

GAMES FOR GREAT HALLS

Look Behind You

● PLAYERS:

4 OR MORE

● SUPPLIES:

A NERF BALL, DUCT TAPE, TWO TRASH CANS, AND, FOR EACH PERSON, A BASEBALL CAP AND POCKET MIRROR FOR EACH PERSON.

Before playing this game, help kids create their playing caps by attaching pocket mirrors to the bills of baseball caps. Duct tape works well for this. Position the mirrors off to one side so kids can see behind themselves when wearing the caps.

Form two teams. Place trash cans at opposite ends of the room and determine the playing-area boundaries. Explain that teams will compete to get the most goals by tossing the Nerf ball into their trash cans. However, teams must always face away from their own trash cans and use only the mirror to see where to pass the ball or attempt a goal. Players who hold the ball may take no more than three steps before passing or shooting the ball. If one team knocks the ball out of bounds, the other team gets possession.

Begin the game by tossing the ball into play. Then act as referee to keeps kids from crashing into each other and to remind them of the rules. If someone is caught turning around to look at his or her team's goal, give a free over-the-shoulder shot (a few feet away from the goal) to a member of the other team. The first team to make 10 goals wins.

■ **Leader Tip:**

Keep score by writing backward on newsprint so kids can see the score in their mirrors.

O Captain, My Captain

Form two teams and place teams on opposite sides of the room. Have teams each pick a captain and blindfold him or her. Bring the two captains together and flip a coin to determine who is "It."

Explain that the object of the game is for It to tag the other captain by following the directions of his or her teammates. The only catch is that the team players can say only one phrase: "O Captain, my Captain." The captain must decide what the directions mean based on how his or her team says, "O Captain, my Captain."

Tell teams to decide together how they'll say the phrase to mean different things. For example, saying the phrase in a falsetto voice might mean "turn around and run." Or emphasizing the last word might mean "turn right," while emphasizing the first word might mean "turn left." Once teams have worked out a code, start the game. Have the team whose captain is It direct its captain toward the other captain, while that team directs its captain away from It.

Once a captain is tagged, give that team 1 point, change captains, determine who will be It, and play a new round. Continue until everyone has had a chance to be captain.

- **PLAYERS:**

6 OR MORE

- **SUPPLIES:**

TWO BLINDFOLDS AND A COIN.

On-the-Ball Relay

● PLAYERS:

4 OR MORE

● SUPPLIES:

TWO BASKETBALLS, TWO SOCCER BALLS, AND TWO SOFTBALLS.

Make two piles of balls, each with a basketball, a soccer ball, and a softball, at one end of your game room. Form two teams and have them each line up single file across from one pile of balls, at least 30 feet away.

On "go," the first person on each team races to the basketball and tries to balance on top of it for at least two seconds. (You'll need an adult volunteer standing near each team's ball as a safety spotter and timer.) As soon as a racer holds his or her balance for two seconds, he or she races back to tag the next person in line.

After each person on a team has balanced on the basketball, team members must each race to balance on the soccer ball and balance on it for two seconds. Finally, replace the soccer ball with the softball and have kids do the same thing.

The first team to have its last person in line cross the finish line after balancing on the softball wins.

Paper-Product Battle

Form teams of four. Set out the supplies and tell teams to use the cardboard and duct tape to create four pieces of armor: a helmet, a breastplate, leg guards, and a shield. Tell kids that each team member will get one piece of armor to wear during the battle. Give teams each an equal supply of scrap paper for them to wad up and use as "bombs." Also give each team a hat to use as a "crown."

Say: **The object of the game is to defeat the other teams by stealing their crowns. Any team can steal another team's crown when all of that team's players are eliminated. A team player is eliminated when a paper bomb strikes him or her on any exposed area on his or her front side. Strikes on armor or on a player's backside don't count. All paper bombs can be used repeatedly by anyone who finds them. Decide where in the room you want to establish your kingdom (that is, where you want to place your crown), then get together with your team and decide on a strategy for winning the battle.**

When teams are ready, start the battle. The first team to capture all the crowns, or the last team with a surviving member, wins the game.

● **PLAYERS:**

8 OR MORE

● **SUPPLIES:**

CARDBOARD, DUCT TAPE, SCISSORS, SCRAP PAPER OR NEWSPAPERS, AND A HAT FOR EVERY FOUR PEOPLE.

GAMES FOR GREAT HALLS

Ping-Pong Party Race

● **PLAYERS:**

2 OR MORE

● **SUPPLIES:**

TWO PING-PONG BALLS AND A CURLED-BLOWER PARTY FAVOR FOR EACH PERSON.

Set up a winding course in the game room by setting out chairs or other objects to mark the boundaries. Form two teams and give each team a Ping-Pong ball. Have half the members of each team line up at the beginning of the course and half line up at the end. Give kids each a curled-blower party favor and tell them they're going to participate in a relay race in which the goal is to push the Ping-Pong ball through the course by blowing at it through their party favors.

The first person on each team must race the team's ball to the other end of the course, then the second person on each team will race the balls back (and so on for as many people as you have on each team). Tell kids it's permissible to sabotage an opponent's race by blowing his or her ball off-course. But remind them that the object of the game is to win the race—not just to harass the other team.

When teams are ready, start the race. It's OK if kids' balls go off the course. Just direct them to blow the ball back on the track before continuing the race. The first team to finish the race wins.

Plague Pair-Race

Form two teams and give each team a supply of toilet paper. Within each team, form pairs. Gather both teams at one end of the game room and designate a finish line at the other end. In the open space in the middle, place several simple obstacles, such as chairs or benches.

Tell kids the open space in the middle of the room is the "plague zone," and the goal is for teams to move across the plague zone to safety on the other side. But to do this without being infected, they must follow these two guidelines:

- they must travel in pairs, and
- the pairs must be totally encased in protective shielding (toilet paper).

Pairs can help other pairs wrap themselves in toilet paper, except for the last pair to cross, who must do it on their own. If any pair tears their protective cloth while in the plague zone, they are immediately infected and must go to the hospital (the starting line) to recover (rewrap their toilet paper). Then they can try again. The first team to get all of its members safely across the zone wins.

● **PLAYERS:**

8 OR MORE

● **SUPPLIES:**

TOILET PAPER.

GAMES FOR GREAT HALLS

Purple Marbles

● **PLAYERS:**

4 OR MORE

● **SUPPLIES:**

MASKING TAPE, A BOX, 100 MARBLES (10 OF WHICH ARE PURPLE—OR ANOTHER UNIQUE COLOR), AND A PAPER CUP FOR EACH PERSON.

Tell kids you're going to play Purple Marbles. Use masking tape to mark two parallel lines on the floor at one end the room, no more than three feet apart. This is the "catching zone"—the only place kids can stand during the game.

Have kids stand in the catching zone with their paper cups. Hold the marbles in an open box at the other end of the room. Explain that the object of the game is to collect as many marbles as possible as they enter the catching zone. Kids can catch the marbles only by letting them roll into their cups.

Toss all the marbles out of the box toward the catching zone. Have kids scoop up as many marbles as possible. Kids may not use their hands to keep the marbles in the cups and only marbles that are actually in the cups may be counted as points. Kids receive 1 point for every regular marble they catch and 10 points for every purple marble they catch.

For the second round, have kids face away from you and watch for the marbles by looking between their legs. For the third round, have kids close their eyes. After all rounds, the person with the most points wins.

■ **Leader Tip:**

Warn kids to be careful not to step on the marbles while they're catching so they don't slip and fall.

● **GREAT GROUP GAMES**

Slow-Motion Marble Race

Form two teams and give teams each a marble, tape, and a large (but equal) supply of cardboard tubing. Tell teams you're going to hold a slow-motion marble race. Have teams each use their supplies to create a marble track that spans the length of the room. Teams may design their tracks however they like, as long as they follow these two rules:

● the marble must roll without assistance through the entire course, and

● the marble that takes the closest to two minutes to finish its course wins.

Kids may use chairs or any other items to prop up their track as needed. Before starting the race, inspect each track to be sure kids followed the instructions. When everything is ready, start the race. The team whose marble finishes the race nearest to the two-minute time mark wins.

■ Leader Tip:

You may want to hold several races, allowing teams the opportunity to change their track designs between each race.

● **PLAYERS:**

2 OR MORE

● **SUPPLIES:**

TWO SAME-SIZE MARBLES, TAPE, A STOPWATCH (OR WATCH WITH A SECOND HAND), AND LOTS OF CARDBOARD TUBING.

GAMES FOR GREAT HALLS

Games on
the Go

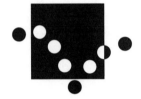

⬛·Aisle Find It!

Arrange to rent or "borrow" a local grocery store for a game of Hide-and-Seek, grocery style. The best time for this is late at night—after the busy hours are over. Check with members of your congregation for people who might be able to arrange the use of a store. Offer to do some kind of service (such as shelving groceries) in return for the use of the store.

For the game, form teams of two to five. Have teams each hide 10 removable stickers somewhere on food displays or racks, then create clues to help other teams find them. For example, someone might place a sticker near a doughnut display and write "They're holey" for a clue.

Have kids write the clues on separate 3×5 cards. Tell them to keep the clue to the first item, then attach the second clue to the first item; the third clue to the second item; and so on. The last item will have no clue attached to it.

Have teams give each other the first clues, then compete to see who can collect another team's clues and stickers first.

● **PLAYERS:**

4 OR MORE

● **SUPPLIES:**

REMOVABLE ADHESIVE STICKERS, 3×5 CARDS, TAPE, AND PENCILS.

GAMES ON THE GO

⬛ Bible Menu Scrabble

● PLAYERS:

2 OR MORE

● SUPPLIES:

A BIBLE AND A PEN
FOR EACH PERSON.

This game will help you fill your waiting time at a restaurant with fun. While your kids are waiting for the food to arrive, challenge them to a game of Bible Menu Scrabble. Give each person a Bible and a pen. Pick a well-known Bible verse, such as John 3:16 or Philippians 4:8. Then challenge kids to come up with a paraphrase of the verse using only those words they can find on their menus. Have them each write their paraphrase on a napkin. After five minutes, have kids read aloud their paraphrases. Then choose a different verse to paraphrase.

■ Leader Tip:

For more challenging fun, have someone pick a particularly difficult verse and instruct kids to paraphrase it from the menu in one minute or less.

Bus Concentration

Kids form a human game board in this travel version of *Concentration.*

Create "concentration cards" by drawing matching symbols or words. Make at least 10 matching pairs.

Distribute sheets of blue and red paper. Have kids fold their sheets into "hats" to be used during the game.

Form two teams. Designate one team as the "blue" team and the other as the "red" team. Have a volunteer from each team move to the front seats. Shuffle the concentration cards and distribute them to the rest of the kids. Make sure you've distributed both cards in each matching pair. Don't let the volunteers see the cards.

Have the blue team's volunteer call out two names. Have those two people show their cards to the volunteers. If their cards match, they must each wear blue hats. If their cards don't match, they must turn them back over. Then the red team's volunteer calls out two names and tries to get a match. Continue until all the cards are matched.

Count up the red and blue hats to determine the winning team. Play several rounds, mixing up the concentration cards and choosing different volunteers each time.

■ **Leader Tip:**

If you have fewer than 10 kids, have kids each hold two cards. Then, when the players call out a name, they'll also have to call "right hand" or "left hand."

● **PLAYERS:**

10 OR MORE

● **SUPPLIES:**

BLUE AND RED CONSTRUCTION PAPER, PAPER, AND A MARKER.

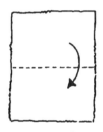

GAMES ON THE GO

·꘍· Crazy Bowling

● **PLAYERS:**

4 OR MORE

● **SUPPLIES:**

NONE.

If you have two groups of kids sharing neighboring lanes at a bowling alley, you can play these bowling variations:

● **Copycat Bowling**—Form two teams (teams should be in adjoining lanes). Have a player from one of the teams bowl one ball. Then, have a player from the other team attempt to knock down the same number of pins as the first team's player. Give 1 point if the person on team 2 is within one pin, 5 if he or she knocks down the same number of pins, and 10 if he or she knocks down exactly the same pins. Have kids roll the second ball in each frame just for fun. Alternate which team goes first in a frame until everyone has bowled. Ignore the regular scoring system and tally the copycat points instead.

● **Weird Bowling**—Have kids compete to see who can create the strangest bowling motion. Have kids score their teammates from 1 to 10 for originality. Add these points to that person's final bowling score before determining the overall bowling champ.

● **Siamese Bowling**—Have kids pair off and bowl as a pair during the game. Have them do this by sharing each turn. For example, if one partner knocks over three pins on his or her first shot, have the other partner try to make the spare.

·🎲·Guess the Distance

Form teams of no more than four and give everyone 3×5 cards and pens.

While driving to your destination, call out objects (such as signs, bridges, and buildings) in the distance and have each team member silently guess the distance in tenths of miles to those objects. Have kids write down their guesses on the 3×5 cards.

Using your vehicle's odometer, measure the distance from the time you call out the object until the car passes the object. Then add up the difference between the actual mileage and each group member's guess to determine that group's score. For example:

● if a team's guesses on a particular distance were 3.0, 1.5, 1.0, and 1.0,

● and the actual distance was 1.2 miles, then

● that team's score would be 1.8 + 0.3 + 0.2 + 0.2 = 2.5.

Play at least five rounds, adding up the scores each time. The team with the lowest score wins.

● **PLAYERS:**

4 OR MORE

● **SUPPLIES:**

PENS AND 3×5 CARDS.

GAMES ON THE GO

Hello-Goodbye Game

● PLAYERS:

3 OR MORE

● SUPPLIES:

SMALL TREATS, SUCH AS HERSHEY'S KISSES.

This brain teaser can be played any-where—on the bus or in a fast-food restaurant. Gather kids together and tell them you're going to play the Hello-Goodbye Game. Do your best Queen Elizabeth imitation and wave "royally" at various people in the group, saying, "Hello. Goodbye."

After you've waved to several people, ask, "Who'd I wave to?" Kids will respond by naming one of the people you aimed your wave at. But the trick of the game is this: The first person to speak or make a noise after you ask, "Who'd I wave to?" becomes the person you actually "waved to."

So, for example, if you aimed your wave at Sara, then asked, "Who'd I wave to?" and Karen popped up and said "Sara," you'd say, "No, I waved at you." Give a small treat, such as a Hershey's Kiss, to the first person to correctly guess who you "waved to."

Don't give any explanation about the method to your madness. Just repeat the game until somebody catches on. When a few kids finally do figure out the pattern, tell them not to say anything but to try the Hello-Goodbye Game themselves. That way you'll know whether they've actually figured it out. Continue until everyone has figured out the game.

Honk if You Love . . .

This is a good game to play while traveling on busy highways. Form teams and have each team create a sign to show to 10 different cars you pass—or that pass you—on the highway. Have teams design their signs to entice passing drivers to honk their horns. All signs must be in good taste.

For example, teams might create a sign that reads "Honk if you love chocolate" or "Honk if you love the Chicago Bulls." Award the team that gets the most honks an ice cream or soft drink treat at the next rest stop.

● **PLAYERS:**

2 OR MORE

● **SUPPLIES:**

CARDBOARD AND MARKERS.

Hot-Banana Talks

Before leaving on a long trip, have kids come up with 10 or 15 questions they'd like to ask each other. Suggest questions that are serious, such as "What's most important to you in life?" and questions that aren't so serious, such as "If you were an insect, which insect would you be and why?" Screen the questions to make sure none are too embarrassing. Then write each on a slip of paper and put them into a sack.

During the trip, give kids a banana and have them toss it around while music plays on the radio (like in the game Hot Potato). At random intervals, turn off the music and call out "stop." Each time you call "stop," the person holding the banana must answer a question from the sack. Repeat the process for the next question. After kids get the hang of the game, have them write new questions and play again.

⚡·I've Got a Problem

Form pairs or trios. Give groups each a study Bible or a Bible and a pocket concordance. Start the game by saying, "I've got a problem..." Then describe a typical problem teenagers face, such as "My parents won't let me stay out late" or "My girlfriend is pressuring me to have sex."

Give kids no more than three minutes to search for Bible passages that say something about the issue or give advice for dealing with the problem. After three minutes, have kids each read their verse or verses and allow the other groups to discuss whether they think the verses apply to the situation.

Allow different people to determine the problem for each round. This game doesn't require a scorekeeper, but it may need redirection once in a while if kids misinterpret a verse.

● **PLAYERS:**

4 OR MORE

● **SUPPLIES:**

BIBLES AND POCKET CONCORDANCES.

·License for Fun

● **PLAYERS:**

2 OR MORE

● **SUPPLIES:**

NONE NEEDED.

Form teams of no more than four. Have teams each choose a number from zero to nine and two letters from A to Z. Teams may not choose the same numbers or letters.

During a specified number of miles, have teams accumulate points by looking for their chosen letters and numbers on the license plates of passing cars and trucks. Each time a team's number or letter appears on a license plate, the team gets 10 points. Teams get 20 bonus points if both of their letters—or their number and any one letter—appear on the same plate. Teams get 50 bonus points if all three appear on the same plate.

Determine the number of miles you'll play and help kids keep score. The team accumulating the most points wins. Have kids agree on a reward for the winning team (such as first choice for snacks or soft drinks at the next rest stop).

•📐•Musical Hats

Ask kids each to wear a hat in the car, van, or bus when you go on a road trip. At some point on the trip, tell kids you're going to play Musical Hats. Have kids gather in a rough circle—close enough so they can reach the people on either side of them. Have kids vote on who has the silliest hat, then remove that hat from the circle. Then have kids practice passing their hats in unison around the circle from head to head.

Now you're ready to play the game. Sit next to the stereo or CD player controls. Whenever you play the music, have kids start passing the hats from head to head. Whenever the music stops, the person left without a hat on must leave the game. Remove one more hat from the circle, then continue the game (possibly changing the style of music by switching the radio station). Keep playing until only one person remains.

• PLAYERS:

3 OR MORE

• SUPPLIES:

A HAT FOR EACH PERSON AND A CAR STEREO OR CD PLAYER.

GAMES ON THE GO

⬛ Name That Laugh

● PLAYERS:

4 OR MORE

● SUPPLIES:

A TAPE RECORDER WITH A TAPE COUNTER AND A BUILT-IN MICRO-PHONE, A PAD OF PAPER, AND A PEN-CIL.

Before your next trip, secretly ask each person to laugh into your tape recorder. Note what number the tape counter is on before you record each person. Write each person's name on your pad, in order, as he or she laughs into your recorder. Next to each name, write the tape-counter number you noted before you recorded that person.

While your group is on the road, play a round of Name That Laugh. Advance or rewind to one of the tape-counter numbers on your pad. Play the laugh, then ask the group to vote on who they think the laugher is. Whoever wins the vote must then laugh on the spot for all to hear. Play the tape-recorded laugh again, then announce the laugher's true identity. Keep going until every laugher has been identified.

● GREAT GROUP GAMES

·⬚·One to 20

Form teams of no more than four for this unique scavenger hunt. For this hunt, kids will make up their own lists as they go.

Give teams each a sheet of paper and a pencil and have them number from one to 20 along the left side. Then say: **In this scavenger hunt, you must go from house to house and collect an increasing number of items from each house. For example, you can collect any one item at the first house and list that item on your paper. Then at the second house, you must collect two identical items (such as paper clips or candy bars) and list what you got on your paper. Continue until you collect 20 identical items at the final house. Then return.**

The first team to return with its items gets 5 bonus points. Then teams each get 1 point for collecting items that no other group collected. For example, if one group collects 15 pennies and another collects 10 pennies, neither team gets a point for their pennies—only unique items win points.

■ Leader Tip:

If it seems unsafe to send kids from house to house, try getting families from the church to volunteer their homes. Or simply send kids around the church grounds to collect their items.

● PLAYERS:

4 OR MORE

● SUPPLIES:

PAPER AND PEN-CILS.

GAMES ON THE GO

Passing Duelers

● PLAYERS:

12 OR MORE

● SUPPLIES:

EQUAL NUMBERS OF MARBLES, COTTON BALLS, AND PAPER CLIPS.

Form two teams (kids will need to sit near their teammates). Distribute equal numbers of marbles, cotton balls, and paper clips to each team. Have each person on a team take one item. Explain the value of the items as follows:

- marbles—8 points
- cotton balls—4 points
- paper clips—2 points

Say: **The object of this game is to win the most points. When I say "pass," you must quickly and secretly pass your items among your teammates. You may hold only one item at a time. When I say "stop," you must keep the item you're holding out of view of the other team. At that time, any person may challenge any member of the other team to a "duel."**

In a duel, the players show the items they're holding at the same time, and a winner is determined. If the item you're holding is of a higher value than the item held by your opponent, you win your point value plus their point value for your team. If the items are of identical value, both teams win the point value of the item. If your item has a lower value than your opponent's, the other team wins the point value of both items.

Allow only three duels per round. Play enough rounds so everyone has plenty of chances to duel.

● **GREAT GROUP GAMES**

Photo Quest

Form groups of five. Be sure each group has a responsible driver and a camera with a fresh 12-exposure roll of film.

Give groups 45 minutes to go into your community and take the strangest photos they possibly can. The only rules are that the photos must be in good taste, show concern for safety, and include at least one group member in each photo (all group members must be in at least one picture). Some strange photo ideas to get kids started might include:

● group members sticking out their tongues at a community statue,

● group members posing with chopsticks in a strange configuration outside a Chinese restaurant, or

● group members posing in odd arrangements while swinging at a local park.

At the appointed time, have a volunteer take the rolls of film to a one-hour developer. During the waiting time, play games or enjoy food at your church. Then, have someone bring the developed prints back to church for the kids to rank from most to least strange. Award 1 point for the least strange photo and increasingly more points for each better photo. Total the points by team and award a prize to the winning team.

● **PLAYERS:**

10 OR MORE

● **SUPPLIES:**

A CAMERA WITH FILM AND A CAR FOR EVERY FIVE PEOPLE. YOU'LL ALSO NEED A PRIZE FOR THE WINNING TEAM.

GAMES ON THE GO

Rest-Stop Keep Away

• PLAYERS:

6 OR MORE

• SUPPLIES:

TWO FOOTBALLS OR FLYING DISKS.

Form two equal teams before you stop at a rest stop. Give each team a football or a flying disk. Say: **The object of this game is for your team to be holding both footballs (or flying disks) when I call everyone back to the van. You may not run more than five steps with the ball, and you may not steal it away from another player. You must pass the ball to teammates while trying to intercept their ball at the same time.**

Don't tell kids how long you'll be at the rest stop. When they've had sufficient time to stretch their legs in this game, call them back to the van and determine a winner (if any). Keep the same teams for long trips and see which ends up with the most wins throughout the trip.

Secret Map Messages

Here's a great mystery game for those hours on the road. Form pairs and give each pair a pencil and a map section. Any state or national map section will work, just make sure everyone's map section is the same.

On your own map section, draw a simple symbol, number, or short word. Make sure you make the item large enough to be easily recognized from a distance. Note which towns and landmarks your secret item intersects, then use them to create a "connect-the-dots" pattern that'll reproduce your secret drawing.

Randomly call out to kids the names of those locations that intersect your drawing. Have pairs race to be the first to reproduce the secret item on their own maps by locating the places you name and discovering the pattern that connects them. The first pair to identify the symbol, number, or word wins.

● **SUPPLIES:**

A PENCIL AND IDENTICAL COPIES OF A STATE OR NATIONAL MAP SECTION FOR EVERY TWO PEOPLE.

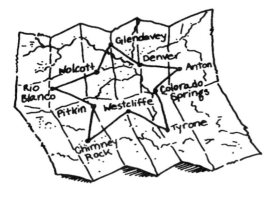

GAMES ON THE GO

Storytelling Travel Game

• PLAYERS:

4 OR MORE

• SUPPLIES:

NONE NEEDED.

This game works well for creative kids who're cooped up in a car or van for long trips. Tell kids you're going to create a story together. To begin, have one person volunteer as the storyteller, then assign three other people to each come up with one of these story elements:

- the main character, including his, her, or its name;
- the setting; and
- the opening line of the story.

The storyteller must use these elements to begin telling a story. Every one or two minutes, have another person take up the story line, shaping it however he or she wants. After several people have told part of the story, call time and have one other person create the ending to the story.

For fun, you can take notes of the stories kids create and include them in a youth group scrapbook or put them in the youth newsletter.

·🎲·Themes

Before a long trip, have kids catch up on their TV show themes. Encourage pairs or trios to watch a few popular and not so popular shows and practice humming the theme songs or music to the shows. Then have groups record themselves humming four or five of their favorites. Have groups bring these tapes along for a guessing game on the bus or van.

Have groups each play one theme song at a time and see how long it takes for the other groups to guess the name of the show, the day and time it airs, and one main character's name.

● **PLAYERS:**

4 OR MORE

● **SUPPLIES:**

A TAPE PLAYER.

GAMES ON THE GO

·🎲·Tilly Green

Here's another brain teaser to make long trips interesting and fun. Tell kids you want to tell them about Tilly Green, a good friend of yours. Explain that if you tell them enough about Tilly Green, they'll come to know her just as you do.

Tell kids about Tilly Green by explaining to them what Tilly Green likes and what she doesn't like. For example, you might say, "Tilly Green loves apples, but she hates oranges" or "Tilly Green likes doors, but she hates windows."

The trick is this: Tilly Green loves anything that is spelled with one or more double letters; for example, "Tilly Green hates California, but she absolutely adores Mississippi, and she's quite fond of Tennessee." You can even say things such as "Tilly Green loves swimming, but she hates the water" or "She hates storms, but she loves hurricanes and typhoons." As kids catch on to the secret, have them join in by talking about Tilly Green until others catch on, too.

Van Scavenger Hunt

This hunt works well when taking a group on an extended trip out of town. Create a list of items that can likely be found on a van, car, or bus in which your group is traveling. Some suggestions are listed below to get you started but feel free to add your own:

- lint
- a green man (such as on a dollar bill)
- a penny from the '80s
- a lipstick mustache
- two socks tied in a knot
- a list of ingredients
- three pairs of anything

Form teams of two or more. On the van (or whatever you're traveling in), call out the items one at a time and have teams race to find them. The first team to come up with the item wins a point. Award the winners with soft drinks at your next pit stop.

● **PLAYERS:**

4 OR MORE

● **SUPPLIES:**

NONE NEEDED.

GAMES ON THE GO

Verse Search

• PLAYERS:

2 OR MORE

• SUPPLIES:

A BIBLE.

While traveling through towns with your youth group, have them play this Bible-verse search game. Choose a number of Bible verses that don't have any obscure or archaic words. Using a translation such as the NIV or the NCV should help.

For example, you might choose Romans 12:4, which reads: "Each one of us has a body with many parts, and these parts all have different uses" (NCV). As kids look around at signs and billboards, have them race to point out the words from the verse in sentence order. Kids may also point out pictures that represent words (such as a picture of a body for the word "body"). Have kids choose a person to be the judge who will evaluate whether the words or pictures group members find are valid for the verse.

·⚅·Word Relay

Form a circle and tell kids you're going to play Word Relay. Explain that the object of the game is to create the longest sentence possible and to avoid being the person who names the last word in a sentence. Each person can contribute only one word.

For example, the first person can start with any word he or she wants—anything from "the" to "every" to "dinosaurs." The next person must then add a word that continues the sentence without completing it. For example, if the first word were "dinosaurs," the next person might add the word "that." He or she could not say "eat" or "roam," however, because both of those verbs would create a complete sentence: "Dinosaurs eat" or "Dinosaurs roam." Each person who ends a sentence gets 1 point. The object is to finish the game with as few points as possible.

● **PLAYERS:**

2 OR MORE

● **SUPPLIES:**

NONE NEEDED.

Games for
the Great
Outdoors

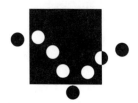

Ant Antagonists

Form two ant "colonies" and have each colony choose a "queen" (it doesn't have to be a girl!). Make sure your colonies have roughly equal numbers of guys and girls. Have each queen put on the oversize sweat clothes, then have team members stuff the queen with as many inflated balloons as possible. These are the queen's "eggs."

After the queens are stuffed, have each person stuff one inflated balloon up the back of his or her shirt. This is the player's "life essence." Tell colonies each that the object of the game is to move their queen in to "take over" the other queen's chamber with at least three of her "eggs" still in place. At the same time, colonies must try to eliminate the opposing team's queen by "popping" all her eggs and wiping out her colony.

Team members are eliminated when their balloons are popped. The queen is eliminated only after all of her balloons are popped. But the only way to pop anyone's balloon—including the queen's—is by hugging. During the game, kids can hug only same-sex "ants"—except for the queen. Anyone can hug the queen.

Once kids understand the rules, designate the queen's chamber for each team, then start the game. The first queen to reach the other queen's chamber with at least three eggs intact wins.

● **PLAYERS:**

20 OR MORE

● **SUPPLIES:**

BALLOONS AND TWO SETS OF OVER-SIZED SWEAT CLOTHES.

Catapult Archery

● PLAYERS:

2 OR MORE

● SUPPLIES:

TWO LARGE STATIONARY POLES (ABOUT FIVE FEET APART), SURGICAL TUBING, AN OLD FOOTBALL (CUT IN HALF), AN EMPTY REFRIGERATOR BOX, AND WATER BALLOONS.

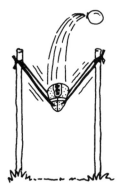

This is a great event to include in your next Crazy Summer Olympics. In an open field, set out an empty refrigerator box on its end. About 40 feet away, plant two poles firmly in the ground, about five feet apart.

Cut an old football in half and punch two holes in the pointed end of one half. Save the other half to use as a replacement, if necessary. Thread a long strand of surgical tubing through those holes. (You can get surgical tubing from most hospitals, army-surplus stores, or pharmaceutical-supply stores.) Then attach each end of the strand to a pole to create a supersize slingshot.

Hold an "archery" contest to see who can knock over the box the most times with a given number of water balloons. Have kids fire the water balloons by placing them in the football "pouch," pulling the strand back, and then releasing. It will take a few tries for kids to get the feel of the catapult, so allow a few practice shots for each person.

Each time a person knocks over the box, give him or her 10 points. The person with the most points after firing five balloons wins.

Caterpillar Tag

Choose three or four people to be "It." Whenever an It tags anyone, that person must join It by placing his or her hands on Its waist, forming a line. Now both players try to tag another.

When all players have been joined to one of the It lines, call out **"Caterpillar tag!"** and point to one of the lines. That line then becomes the caterpillar.

The caterpillar tries to tag anyone in the other lines. Whenever another line is tagged, those kids must link up with the caterpillar and begin chasing the lines that remain. The game is over when everyone has become a part of the caterpillar.

■ Leader Tip:

As a fun variation at the end of this game, have the caterpillar chase its own tail. Then the game is over when the caterpillar becomes a circle of kids.

● **PLAYERS:**

15 OR MORE

● **SUPPLIES:**

NONE NEEDED.

GAMES FOR THE GREAT OUTDOORS

Disk-Douser Relay

● **PLAYERS:**

12 OR MORE

● **SUPPLIES:**

FOUR BUCKETS OF WATER, 24 SPONGES, AND A FLYING DISK FOR EACH PERSON.

Set up a relay race area with a starting line at least 100 feet from the relay line. At the relay line, place chairs or other objects for participants to run around before heading back to the starting line. You'll need access to water, so plan the location accordingly.

Set up four buckets of water, two on either side of the racing area. Place six sponges in each bucket. Form teams of four. Have one team begin as the "dousers" and the others line up at the starting line. Give each person on a team a flying disk to wear on top of his or her head.

On "go," the first people on each team must race to the relay line, circle the chair, and return back to the start for the next person to go. The dousers will attempt to knock the flying disks off the racers with the water-laden sponges. Kids may not hold onto their "hats" while running.

The douser team gets 2 points for each disk they knock off. The racing teams get 1 point each time a racer gets back to the start with the disk still on. And whichever team gets all its members back first earns an additional 2 points.

Rotate so all teams a chance to be the dousers. The team with the most points at the end wins.

Dodge Ball in the Round

Have players form two circles, one inside the other. Tell kids in the inner circle to join hands and run or skip around clockwise.

Toss the kickball to the kids in the outer circle. Tell them the object of the game is to use the ball to try to hit the legs of the players in the inner circle. When a player is hit, he or she joins the outer circle and continues to play. Inner circle players may jump, run, or open their legs, but they may not break the circle. If someone from the outer circle tosses the ball and hits someone above the waist, the outer circle person must join the inner circle. The game is over when all the inside players have joined the outer circle.

Repeat the game, having the original teams switch roles.

● **PLAYERS:**

15 OR MORE

● **SUPPLIES:**

A KICKBALL.

GAMES FOR THE GREAT OUTDOORS

Four-Headed Soccer

• PLAYERS:

48 OR MORE

• SUPPLIES:

ROPE, A SOCCER BALL, AND A SOCCER FIELD. YOU'LL ALSO NEED COLORED ARMBANDS TO DISTINGUISH ONE TEAM FROM ANOTHER.

Here's a great outdoor game to play with a large group of kids. Form two teams and give each team a different armband color. Within each team, have kids form groups of four. Give each group of four a supply of rope, then have foursomes tie their ankles together so they form a square facing outward.

Once all the foursomes are tied together, take kids out to the soccer field and play a regular game of soccer, with each foursome acting as one player. (Tell foursomes to lock arms while they're playing. This will give them greater stability.) All the regular rules for soccer apply.

The team that scores the most goals during the game wins.

▰·Game in a Box

F orm pairs and give each pair a refrigerator box. Have kids create their "game suits" using the boxes (see the illustration below). Encourage kids to decorate their boxes any way they choose.

When the game suits are complete, determine which variation of the game you'll play (see instructions below). Then form teams and start playing. During this game, kids will need to work together to keep from tearing their box and to keep the other team from scoring. Here are a few games to consider:

● **Same-Team-in-a-Box Option**— Form two teams and have pairs from each team wear a game suit together. During this game, the goal is to toss around a small playground ball and score goals in the goal holes on the back of opposing team members' game suits. Again, see illustration for the location of the goals.

● **Opposing-Teams-in-a-Box Option**—Form two teams. For this game, use the same basic rules as the first game, only instead of having pairs from the same team share a box, have one member of each team stand inside each game suit. Players may not steal the ball from an opponent in the same game suit. They may, however, attempt to block a pass or turn the game suit so the person doesn't make a good pass or shot.

Play to a set score—or until the refrigerator boxes are ready for recycling.

● **PLAYERS:**

8 OR MORE

● **SUPPLIES:**

A REFRIGERATOR BOX FOR EVERY TWO PEOPLE, SCISSORS, AND MARKERS.

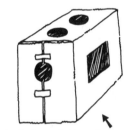

Cut hole on bottom for legs.

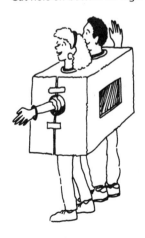

GAMES FOR THE GREAT OUTDOORS

Hoop Tossers

● PLAYERS:

8 OR MORE

● SUPPLIES:

A HULA-HOOP AND AN OLD SHEET FOR EVERY FOUR PEOPLE. YOU'LL ALSO NEED NYLON ROPE AND A SUPPLY OF LARGE, PLASTIC BALLS OR PLAYGROUND BALLS.

Before the game, have kids help you make enough hoop tossers for each team of two to four to have one. A hoop tosser is made by spreading an old sheet across the inside of a Hula-Hoop. Have kids attach the cloth by winding a nylon rope around the hoop and through holes cut on the edge of the cloth. Tell kids not to make the cloth too tight across the hoop—it'll need some "give" for them to catch a ball in it.

When you're ready to play, toss out several balls and choose one of the following game variations:

● **High Toss**—Have teams hold their hoop tossers and attempt to toss the balls as high as possible by lowering the hoops to the ground, then rapidly moving them upward. See how many times each team can keep the ball bouncing without allowing it to hit the ground.

● **Hoop-Tosser Duels**—Give teams each a hoop tosser and a ball. Have them use their hoop tossers to steal balls from as many other teams as possible. Tell teams they can use only their hoop tossers to "scoop" balls away from others, but they must also bounce their own ball(s) at least once every 10 seconds. The team with the most balls when time is called wins.

● **Tossers in the Round**—Have teams pick names for themselves, then form a rough circle. As one team tosses the ball, call out another team's name—that team must run to catch the ball.

● **GREAT GROUP GAMES**

Get the Message

Form teams of no more than four. Have one person on each team stand at one end of a large field. These people will be the receivers. Have the other team members stand at the opposite end of the field (at least 50 feet away). These are the senders.

Explain that the object of the game is for the senders to relay a short message to the receivers and for the receivers to be the first to follow the message's instruction.

Instructions could be anything from "flip" to "shout." Keep instructions down to three words or fewer and have different teams each choose a different message to send.

Explain that the senders may not speak or do the action but that they must form themselves into letters to spell the message for the receivers to read. They can do this either standing up or lying down on the ground. When the receiver understands the message, he or she must do the action before the other teams complete their actions. If the action was correct, that team wins the round.

Play more than one round so kids each have a chance to be the receivers.

● **PLAYERS:**

8 OR MORE

● **SUPPLIES:**

NONE NEEDED.

GAMES FOR THE GREAT OUTDOORS

Greased-Watermelon Herding

● PLAYERS:

12 OR MORE

● SUPPLIES:

A SWIMMING POOL, 10 WATER-MELONS, AND A TUB OF LARD.

Form two teams and assign each team a different side of the swimming pool to be its "corral." Set out the watermelons and generously coat each with the lard. Then toss the melons in the pool (they'll float).

Tell kids that the object of the game is simply to "herd" the watermelons safely up onto the their team's side of the pool. The only rules are that the watermelons may not be thrown, and no one may leave the pool during the game. Each time a team herds a watermelon to its corral, that team gets one point. If a team breaks a watermelon, it's penalized 3 points. The team that successfully herds the most watermelons to its corral wins.

After the game, have both teams celebrate by eating the watermelons.

Human Foosball

Form two teams and have teams arrange themselves on the soccer field as if they were players on a Foosball table (see the diagram below).

Once teams are in position, tell kids they're going to play a game of Human Foosball. Just like in real Foosball, players may move freely to the right or to the left, but they may not move forward or backward at any time. The object of the game is to kick the ball into the opponent's goal. If a ball is kicked out of bounds, it is simply tossed back into the game by any player.

Once kids understand the rules, start the game. The first team to score 10 goals wins.

● **PLAYERS:**

30 OR MORE

● **SUPPLIES:**

A SOCCER BALL.

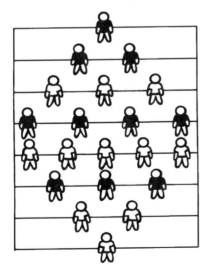

·■·Night Spies

• PLAYERS:

8 OR MORE

• SUPPLIES:

A FLASHLIGHT AND AN IDENTICAL CHILDREN'S PUZZLE FOR EVERY FOUR PEOPLE, AND A MARKER. YOU'LL ALSO NEED A "TREASURE," SUCH AS A CAKE OR A BAG OF CANDY.

Here's a fun, nighttime, treasure hunt game. Before your meeting, ask several adult volunteers to act as "secret agents."

On the back of each completed children's puzzle, write out the location of the "treasure." Plant your camouflaged secret agents in a wooded area and give them each a different set of all the same pieces from the puzzles. Tell the agents to move around constantly but not to give out any of their puzzle pieces unless they are surrounded by a team of young people.

With the young people, form teams of four and give each team a flashlight. Tell teams their goal is to locate each secret agent hiding in the woods, surround him or her, and receive a piece of the puzzle. Once teams have all the puzzle pieces, they can read the message on the back and race to retrieve the treasure from its hiding place.

Warn teams that they may not touch the secret agents and that the only way to get the clues from them is to completely surround them.

When teams are ready, start the game. The first team to get all the puzzle pieces and retrieve the treasure wins.

Four-Way Tug of War

This is a good game to play in late spring, when the weather's beginning to warm up, but fields are still muddy.

Form four teams. Take two equal lengths of rope and tie them together at their midpoints, creating an X shape. Station each team along a different edge of the muddy area and give each team one end of the four-way rope.

On "go," have teams pull on the rope with all their might. The last team to fall in the mud wins.

■ Leader Tip:

You may have to adjust the lengths of some sections of the rope depending on the size and shape of the muddy area.

● **PLAYERS:**

12 OR MORE

● **SUPPLIES:**

ROPE AND A MUDDY AREA.

GAMES FOR THE GREAT OUTDOORS

Sky Raiders

PLAYERS:

8 OR MORE

SUPPLIES:

A HELIUM TANK, SEVERAL HUNDRED FEET OF STRING, AND BALLOONS (WHITE, YELLOW, BLUE, AND BLACK). YOU'LL ALSO NEED A FLASHLIGHT FOR EVERY FOUR PEOPLE.

This game works best on a clear, still night.

Before kids arrive, inflate an equal number of white, yellow, blue, and black balloons with helium. Attach each balloon to a long section of string (20 to 40 feet), then tie the balloons to various objects within the game zone. Attach a few of the white balloons to stones on the ground but tie most balloons to trees. Make sure the balloons rise above the height of the trees they're attached to.

After kids arrive, take them inside and form teams of four. Give each foursome a flashlight. Tell teams their goal is to locate the balloons and return them to the base unpopped. Warn kids that other teams can try to pop or steal their balloons once they have them, so the sooner they return them to base, the better chance they have of getting the points.

Here's how much each balloon color is worth:

- white—50 points
- yellow—75 points
- blue—150 points
- black—400 points

Once teams understand the rules, send them out into the night to retrieve the balloons. The game is over when all the balloons have been accounted for—or at the end of two hours.

Slingshot Keep Away

orm two teams and gather both teams on an open field. Stuff a tennis ball into the end of a long tube sock and swing it around "slingshot" style to show kids how to throw it. On "go," toss the "slingshot" up into the air and let team members race to get it.

Have players try to keep the slingshot away from members of the other team by passing it from teammate to teammate. Each person who holds the slingshot must throw it within 10 seconds, or it is automatically given to the other team.

Award teams 1 point each time a member completes a pass to a teammate or intercepts a pass from an opposing team member. When kids have played themselves out, call time. The team with the most points at the end of the game wins.

● **PLAYERS:**

4 OR MORE

● **SUPPLIES:**

A LONG TUBE SOCK AND A TENNIS BALL.

▪️∙Sock It to Me

● **PLAYERS:**

4 OR MORE

● **SUPPLIES:**

TUBE SOCKS AND FLOUR.

Fill the ends of tube socks with flour. Give kids each a flour-filled tube sock and send them out into a field. Tell them they have five minutes to completely cover everyone in flour by "socking" them with the tube sock. The person with the least flour on his or her body at the end of five minutes wins the round.

Have kids play several rounds, giving them time to dust themselves off between each round.

■ **Leader Tip:**

Breathing the dust from the flour might cause a problem for kids with asthma. Ask these kids to serve as cheerleaders or judges.

Square Races

For this game, choose a grassy area where you've got lots of room. Form teams of two or more and determine a starting place.

Scatter all the cloth strips around the playing area, at least 100 feet from the starting place and a long distance from each other.

Give teams each a specific number of cardboard squares depending on the number of team members. Make sure the squares are no smaller than 6×6 inches and no larger than 12×12 inches. Use the following chart to determine how many squares to give to each team:

Tell kids the object of the game is to collect their teams' cloths and return them to the starting place. They may send one player at a time or all go out as a team to get these cloths, but they must step only on the cardboard and not the ground. Kids may toss the cardboard ahead of themselves to step on or hold them on their feet as they walk.

Challenge kids to be creative and work together to figure how to get the cloths the fastest. If kids touch the ground with their feet, send them back to the starting line to begin again. The first team to recover all of its cloths wins.

● **PLAYERS:**

4 OR MORE

● **SUPPLIES:**

FIVE STRIPS OF CLOTH FOR EACH TEAM—DIFFERENT COLORS FOR DIFFERENT TEAMS— AND A SUPPLY OF CARDBOARD SQUARES (SEE CHART BELOW).

Team Members	Number of Squares
2	3
3	4
4	6
5	8
6 OR MORE	10

Touch and Go

PLAYERS:

3 OR MORE

SUPPLIES:

TEN TO 15 TIRES OR EMPTY BOXES.

In an open field, lay out a "leaping" course with tires or boxes. Set out the items one at a time, with both short and long distances between them. The first few distances can be easy steps but make the distances larger and larger as the course progresses. Make sure even the largest distance in the course is "leapable" for kids.

Gather kids at the starting point and have the first "leaper" try to complete the course by leaping from item to item. The leaper may not touch the ground at any time. If the leaper does touch the ground, or fails to make a "leap," then that person becomes stranded and must be rescued by the next person in line.

If the next leaper makes it further along than the first leaper, then he or she can touch that person while passing by. The first leaper is then freed to go along as far as the second leaper goes. Each player tries to touch and free people as he or she leaps through the course. If necessary, kids can go through the course more than once in order to rescue others.

The game is over when all the kids have made it through the course, either on their own or with the help of another person.

Trash-Bag Soccer

Form two soccer teams. Play a regular game of soccer but with these changes:
- instead of a soccer ball, use a heavy-weight trash bag filled with balloons;
- instead of allowing kids to kick the ball with their feet, tell them they can use only their knees, torsos, or heads to move the ball; and
- have kids score a goal by pushing the ball over a line instead of kicking it into a goal.

The more inflated the bag, the easier it is to play with. Have several "back up" bags ready in case a bag breaks. The team with the most goals at the end of the game wins.

● **PLAYERS:**

20 OR MORE

● **SUPPLIES:**

SEVERAL HEAVY-WEIGHT TRASH BAGS, BALLOONS, AND A SOCCER FIELD.

GAMES FOR THE GREAT OUTDOORS

Tubular Olympics

● **PLAYERS:**

8 OR MORE

● **SUPPLIES:**

SEVERAL STURDY, 3-TO 4-FOOT-LONG MAILING TUBES. YOU'LL ALSO NEED A FEW SAWS AND MARKERS.

Form teams of four and give each team one tube. Describe the following four events for this activity:

● **Tube-Duo Relay**—Two people at a time stand face to face and place a mailing tube between them (held in place only by their stomachs). Have pairs each traverse a short obstacle course without dropping the tube (or using their hands). If they drop the tube, they must begin again. The fastest time wins.

● **Tube Roll**—This is a relay race in which team members must take turns rolling a tube through a specified course. The first racer uses only his or her head; the second uses only knees; the third, only elbows; and the fourth, only heels.

● **Tube-Top Spin**—All four team members must position the tube on their heads and spin in place three times.

■ **Leader Tip:**

If group members stagger their position, they can hold the tube securely between their heads.

The team that wins the most races overall wins the olympics. When you're done, have kids help you cut each tube into four parts (you'll need a few saws for this). Give kids each a part of their team's tube. Then have kids write on each teammates' tube a positive message they'd like to send to that person.

Waterline Sneak

Have kids each make a poncho out of their plastic bag, then use the duct tape to secure a small towel to their back.

Form three teams. Have two of the teams stand in lines facing each other. Blindfold each of these team members and give them each a cup full of water. Tell the third team that their goal is to get their team members through the "waterline" (the path between the two teams) without getting their towels wet. Team members must go one at a time, and they must remain on their feet at all times. The team players with the cups of water may toss them at any time and in any direction. Their goal is to douse the backs of the walking team's members.

Once the first team has walked the waterline, rotate teams so that a new team has to walk the line. Continue until all three teams have gone through the line. The team with the driest towels wins.

● **PLAYERS:**

15 OR MORE

● **SUPPLIES:**

WATER AND CUPS. YOU'LL ALSO NEED A LARGE PLASTIC BAG, BLINDFOLDS, A SMALL TOWEL, AND DUCT TAPE FOR EACH PERSON.

GAMES FOR THE GREAT OUTDOORS

Waterlogged Softball

● **PLAYERS:**

14 OR MORE

● **SUPPLIES:**

A BEACH BALL AND
A PLASTIC BAT.

Form two teams of seven or more. Inflate a beach ball but fill it partly with water so that it moves erratically. Lay out the bases for a softball diamond (make it about half the size of a regular diamond) and tell kids you're going to play Waterlogged Softball.

All the regular rules for softball apply, except the regular ball has been replaced by a partially water-filled beach ball, and the regular bat has been replaced by a plastic one. Play for as many innings as you like. The team with the most runs in the end wins.

Windbag Olympics

Fill a sturdy, plastic trash bag (the clear ones make the game more colorful) half full of air-inflated balloons and half full of helium-inflated balloons. Then tie the end off and seal it with duct tape.

Depending on the weight of the balloons and the bag, you may need to adjust the number of helium balloons you include. The bag should be heavy enough not to float away but light enough to go for long distances when hit in the air.

Try these crazy outdoor games:

● **Air Soccer**—Form teams for soccer. Make a goal at each end of the field by setting two 6-foot ladders about six feet apart and attaching rope across the top between the ladders. Play air soccer by having kids hit the giant air bag with their heads and shoulders, trying to knock it over the opposing team's rope.

● **Air Toss**—Have teams compete to see who can send the bag highest into the air. Tell kids that they can use any props they can find and that any method of "launching" is acceptable as long as it's safe for group members. Gauge the height attained by measuring the bag against a tree, light pole, or building. The team that sends the bag the highest wins.

● **Air Burial**—Take kids to a local pool or lake and have teams compete to see who can submerge the bag under the water first without damaging it.

● **PLAYERS:**

4 OR MORE

● **SUPPLIES:**

LARGE, CLEAR TRASH BAGS; DUCT TAPE; AIR-FILLED BALLOONS; AND HELIUM-FILLED BALLOONS.

GAMES FOR THE GREAT OUTDOORS

GREAT GROUP GAMES ●

Games for All Kinds of Weather

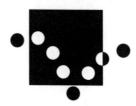

Beach Ball Hockey

Here's an active form of winter fun. Form two hockey teams. Then have kids play a regular game of hockey, except instead of using a puck and hockey sticks, have kids use their fists and an airborne beach ball.

Tell kids the beach ball must remain in the air as long as the ball is in their team's possession. If it touches the ice, the other team then takes possession of the ball at the point where it touched the ice. Also, if kids hit the ball with anything other than their fists or arms, a foul is called and the other team takes possession of the ball at the place the foul was made.

When kids understand the rules, start the game. The team with the most goals at the end of the game wins.

● **PLAYERS:**

20 OR MORE

● **SUPPLIES:**

A FROZEN LAKE OR SKATING RINK, ICE SKATES FOR EACH PERSON, AND A BEACH BALL.

GAMES FOR ALL KINDS OF WEATHER

·🎲· Don't Name Me

● **PLAYERS:**

8 OR MORE

● **SUPPLIES:**

PAPER, TAPE, MARK-
ERS, AND FLASH-
LIGHTS.

This game works great at youth events when you have an unexpected power outage.

Tape a sheet of paper to the back of each person. Give kids each a marker and make the room completely dark. Tell kids the object of the game is to mill around the room and identify the people you encounter, while at the same time trying to conceal your own identity. Kids can do this by disguising their voices, refusing to speak, altering the way they move around the room, or not allowing anyone to touch them.

On the back of each person they encounter, kids must write who they think that person is. Continue the game until it seems most kids have had a chance to write on everyone's back.

Then, by flashlight, check each person's back to see how many people were fooled into thinking he or she was someone else. Award kids a point for each incorrect name written on their sheets. The person who fooled the most people wins.

Don't Douse Your Candle

When your original outdoor activity is rained out, try this challenging but noncompetitive game.

Make sure kids each have a rain poncho—or provide them with plastic trash bag ponchos. Give each person a candle.

Light each person's candle, then send kids out into the rain. Have kids see how long they can keep their candles lit in the rainy weather. If someone's candle goes out, that person must stop and have it relit by the leader, who holds the matches. Continue for three to five minutes or until all the candles have gone out at least once.

■ Leader Tip:

After the game, gather everyone together inside around the lit candles to create a "bonfire" chat. Discuss Matthew 5:14-16. Ask: **How can Christians shine in a world that seems to douse their light?**

● PLAYERS:

3 OR MORE

● SUPPLIES:

CANDLES, MATCHES, AND RAIN GEAR.

Kite Targets

● **PLAYERS:**

6 OR MORE

● **SUPPLIES:**

TWO INEXPENSIVE PLASTIC KITES, STRING, AND TENNIS BALLS.

Next time you have a windy day, get two cheap, plastic kites; some string; and a bunch of tennis balls for this wild activity.

Form two teams and have each team get a kite in the air 25 to 50 feet high. Then give each team two or three tennis balls. The object of the game is to hit the opposing team's kite with a tennis ball to score a point. Downing a kite is worth 10 points.

On "go," have teams see how many points they can score. Kite fliers can attempt to maneuver their kites around the tosses, but they must keep the kites in the air until you call time. After five minutes of tossing, call time and have a new person on each team become the kite flier.

Play until kids have sore arms or until the kites are both grounded.

Champion Bundling

This is a fun game to play on a cold, snowy night when kids arrive bundled up to keep warm. Form two teams and have each team choose a champion. Collect everybody's jackets, coats, mittens, scarves, or any other outerwear they wore to keep warm, and place them all in a pile. On "go," have teams race to "bundle" their champion in as much of the clothing as they can. The team that gets the most items on its champion wins the first round.

For the second round, have the bundled-up champions compete in a simple obstacle course—either inside or outside—which requires them to run, bend over, reach up, and crawl under something. For example, you could have champions run outside, pick up a snowball, strike a target with it, crawl under the target, and then return to home base. The first champion to finish the course wins the second round for his or her team.

For the third round, have kids race to remove the bundled clothing from their champion. The first to do this wins the third round. The team that wins the most rounds wins the game.

● **SUPPLIES:**

NONE NEEDED.

GAMES FOR ALL KINDS OF WEATHER

Rain Catchers

● **PLAYERS:**

6 OR MORE

● **SUPPLIES:**

A LARGE, PLASTIC TRASH BAG FOR EACH PERSON. YOU'LL ALSO NEED A FLYING DISK AND A BUCKET FOR EACH TEAM OF THREE OR MORE.

When heavy spring or summer rains threaten to ruin a perfectly good day of fun for your youth group, try this idea to brighten kids' spirits.

Form two or three teams. Give each team a flying disk and each person a large, plastic trash bag to create a rain poncho. Designate a bucket for each team and set it somewhere out of the rain.

On "go," have team members take turns racing outside, holding the flying disks upside-down on top of their heads. Have kids run around in the rain and collect as much water as possible in the upside-down flying disks, then return and pour the water into their team's bucket. After a specified time limit, compare buckets to see which team has collected the most rain.

■ **Leader Tip:**

Make sure that you don't play this game during an electrical storm. No zaps allowed!

Silent Cake-Bake

Here's a great, active idea for a rainy day. Meet in a home with a large kitchen (or the church kitchen). Supply the ingredients kids will need to make cakes (cake mixes are acceptable). Form teams of three. Tell teams their goal is to create a cake without speaking. Explain that teams must decide what kind of supplies to use and how they'll work together to bake the cake as a team. The only catch is that no one may utter even one word during the whole experience.

When kids understand the rules, begin. The team with the yummiest finished cake wins. After the experience, talk about its challenges. Then enjoy a cake feast and watch a movie together.

● PLAYERS:

6 OR MORE

● SUPPLIES:

A FULLY EQUIPPED KITCHEN, CAKE RECIPES, AND INGREDIENTS OR CAKE MIXES.

Snow-Chariot Races

● **PLAYERS:**

8 OR MORE

● **SUPPLIES:**

LARGE APPLIANCE BOXES, DUCT TAPE, ROPE, AND COLORED MARKERS.

■ **Leader Tip:**

For added fun, give teams a week's notice and have them really use their creativity in building their cardboard snow chariots. Then, on race day, give awards for the most creative snow chariot, the most unusual creation, and the snow chariot that's most likely to survive a blizzard.

After a good snow, have group members meet at a nearby field for snow-chariot races. Provide a large appliance box for each team of four. This is their snow chariot!

Have teams use the duct tape and markers to strengthen and decorate their snow chariots. Then have teams each cut a small hole in the bottom of their creations. Determine which two people will be the pullers, then have them slip one end of a 6-foot rope through the hole, to be held by the other team members who must sit in the box. The pullers will tow their snow chariots across the field.

Go to a snowy field, determine a starting and ending point for the race, and send the cardboard snow chariots off! Kids will soon learn the importance of holding on as the pullers pull away.

For a variation on this race, choose a safe hill for snow chariots (now bobsleds) to race down on gravity power alone.

⬛Soggy Tag

On a wet, summer day when kids want to play in the rain, take them outside for a game of Soggy Tag.

Get out four foam balls (such as Nerf balls)—two of one color and two of another color. Determine the playing area and form two teams. Give one set of same-color foam balls to each team.

The object of the game is to "freeze" the other team by hitting its team members with the foam balls. Teams may throw only their own color of balls and must aim below the waist. Each time someone is hit with an opposing team's foam ball, he or she must freeze in place. Team members may be unfrozen, however, if they're hit or touched with their own team's ball.

Play until one team is completely frozen or until kids are thoroughly soaked.

■ Leader Tip:

One fun way to end this activity is to have kids change into dry clothes, then huddle up to watch a movie together while enjoying some ice cream and soft drinks.

● PLAYERS:

6 OR MORE

● SUPPLIES:

FOUR FOAM BALLS—TWO OF ONE COLOR AND TWO OF ANOTHER COLOR.

GAMES FOR ALL KINDS OF WEATHER

MORE PRACTICAL GAME BOOKS FOR YOUR YOUTH MINISTRY

QUICK CROWDBREAKERS AND GAMES FOR YOUTH GROUPS

Over 200 sure-fire icebreakers guaranteed to get meetings, retreats, and lock-ins off to a lively start...ready in an instant! Taken from "Try This One," a popular section in GROUP Magazine, you'll choose from...

- Pair Games—like Blind Prince Shoe Grab, Cotton Ball Catch, Ice Cream Special, Looks Like Rain;
- Team Tangles—like Autograph Round Up, Jousters, Marshmallow Drop, Name That Hymn, Newspaper Crumple;
- Just for Fun activities—like Church Clues, Close-Up Sounds, Hum That Tune, Laugh Machine, Marching Kazoos;

...and much more. These are creative games perfect for whenever kids get together.

ISBN 0-931529-46-8

HAVE-A-BLAST GAMES FOR YOUTH GROUPS

Here are 101 quick and easy games that will grab kids' attention and require only a few minutes of preparation. Guaranteed to keep your youth group on the ball and energized with icebreakers for meetings, retreats, lock-ins or wherever your group is having a good time. You'll find...

- Crazy Competitions—to build teamwork in your group,
- Remarkable Recreations—to help kids build friendships, and
- Dynamic Diversions—for just plain fun.

Be a creative whiz—the easy way—with *Have-a-Blast Games for Youth Groups*.

ISBN 1-55945-046-0

Order today from your local Christian bookstore, or write:
Group Publishing, P.O. Box 485, Loveland, CO 80539.

INNOVATIVE RESOURCES FOR YOUTH MINISTRY

SHORT SKITS FOR YOUTH MINISTRY

Draw your kids into discussions with more than dry lectures. Each skit packs a significant punch on such teen-friendly topics as...

- sharing faith,
- money,
- marriage,
- world hunger,
- parents,
- nagging,
- sibling rivalry,
- time management.

And each skit is simple to prepare. Assign the parts and let kids create their own characters on the spot. After you've opened the topic for discussion with a skit, use the questions provided to help kids uncover biblical truths on important issues.

Skits are ideal for almost anywhere and for any time. There are no special set requirements—rather, skits use props you already have, such as chairs or a park bench if you're outdoors.

Use these skits to involve kids in growing closer to God.

1-55945-173-4

QUICK SKITS & DISCUSSION STARTERS

Chuck Bolte and Paul McCusker

Grab your kids' attention and encourage their faith to grow. These quick, innovative discussion starters will help your young people...

- build confidence and self-esteem,
- improve their communication skills,
- develop their creative abilities, and
- apply the Bible to their lives.

Plus, you'll save meeting planning time—with easy skits, ready-to-use discussion questions, and relevant Scripture references. Just add a few simple props—and kids—for an unforgettable group experience as you...

- break the ice with 26 ready-to-use warm-up exercises,
- involve young people with 18 complete dramatic sketches,
- challenge your teenagers with thought-provoking questions, and
- strengthen your kids' faith with lively discussions.

ISBN 0-931529-68-9

MORE INNOVATIVE RESOURCES FOR YOUR YOUTH MINISTRY

The Youth Worker's Encyclopedia of Bible-Teaching Ideas: Old Testament/ New Testament

Explore the most comprehensive idea-books available for youth workers! Discover more than 360 creative ideas in each of these 416-page encyclopedias—there's at least one idea for each and every book of the Bible. Find ideas for...retreats and overnighters, learning games, adventures, special projects, parties, prayers, music, devotions, skits, and much more!

Plus, you can use these ideas for groups of all sizes in any setting. Large or small. Sunday or midweek meetings. Bible study. Sunday school class or retreat. Discover exciting new ways to teach each book of the Bible to your youth group.

Old Testament   ISBN 1-55945-184-X
New Testament   ISBN 1-55945-183-1

Clip-Art Cartoons for Churches

Here are over 180 funny, photocopiable illustrations to help you jazz up your calendars, newsletters, posters, fliers, transparencies, postcards, business cards, announcements—all your printed materials! These fun, fresh illustrations cover a variety of church and Christian themes, including church life, Sunday school, youth groups, school life, sermons, church events, volunteers, and more! And there's a variety of artistic styles to choose from so each piece you create will be unique and original.

Each illustration is provided in the sizes you need most, so it's easy to use. You won't find random images here...each image is a complete cartoon. And these cartoons are fun! In fact, they're so entertaining that you may just find yourself reading the book and not photocopying them at all.

Order your copy of **Clip-Art Cartoons for Churches** today...and add some spice to your next printed piece.

ISBN 1-55945-791-0

Bore No More! (For Every Pastor, Speaker, Teacher)

This book is a must for every pastor, youth leader, teacher, and speaker. These 70 audience-grabbing activities pull listeners into your lesson or sermon—and drive your message home!

Discover clever object lessons, creative skits, and readings. Music and celebration ideas. Affirmation activities. All the innovative techniques 85 percent of adult churchgoers say they wish their pastors would try! (recent Group Publishing poll)

Involve your congregation in the learning process! These complete 5- to 15-minute activities highlight common New Testament Lectionary passages, so you'll use this book week after week.

ISBN 1-55945-266-8

Order today from your local Christian bookstore, or write:
Group Publishing, Box 485, Loveland, CO 80539.